grandparents

Translation: Jean Grasso Fitzpatrick

English translation © copyright
1987 by Barron's Educational Series, Inc.

© Parramón Ediciones, S.A.
First Edition, April, 1985
The title of the Spanish edition is *los abuelos*

All inquiries should be addressed to:
Barron's Educational Series, Inc.
250 Wireless Boulevard
Hauppauge, New York 11788

Library of Congress Catalog Card No. 87-11480

International Standard Book No. 0-8120-3853-3

Library of Congress Cataloging-in-Publication Data

Rius, María.
    Grandparents.

    (The Family)
    Translation of: Los abuelos.
    Summary: A simple explanation of what grandparents are
and their place in the family. Includes a guide for
parents and teachers.
    1. Grandparents — Juvenile literature. 2. Family —
Juvenile literature. [1. Grandparents. 2. Family]
I. Parramón, José María. II. Title.
HQ759.9.R5813   1987   306.8′7   87-11480
ISBN 0-8120-3853-3

Legal Deposit: CO-780-87

Printed in Spain by Graficromo
Polígono ''Las Quemadas''
Córboba (España)

7   8   9   9960   9   8   7   6   5   4   3   2   1

the family

grandparents

María Rius

J. M. Parramón

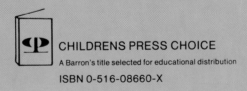

CHILDRENS PRESS CHOICE

A Barron's title selected for educational distribution

ISBN 0-516-08660-X

Each one of your four grandparents started out as a tiny baby…just as you did.

But that was a long, long time ago.

All of them grew up in different places…

and played with their own friends.

When they became adults, each pair of your grandparents…

met ... fell in love ...

and got

married!

And then each pair had a baby. One was *your* mother. The other one was *your* father.

But they were still two families

who lived in different places.

Until one day, when their children met . . . fell in love …

and got married!

And then you were born!

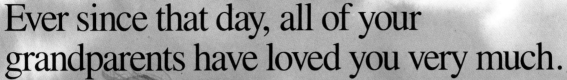

Ever since that day, all of your grandparents have loved you very much.

They like to take you for walks

and tell you stories.

They are sad when they have to say goodbye …

and happy whenever they can come to visit you.

They are your grandparents!

GRANDPARENTS

Grandparents pass on the traditions and customs of their generation, fulfilling a basic function of the family, which is to "transmit from one generation to another the fundamental rules of civilization" (Schroecker).

The four stages of life

During the first twenty years of life, we learn important things by studying, training for a trade or career, and landing our first job. During the next twenty years, we find a home of our own, have children, become established in a career. During the third stage, we try to realize our dreams and dedicate more time to our interests and hobbies, now that our children are grown up and living on their own. Finally, during the last twenty years or so, we reach the "golden years," which can be the best or worst of our lives, depending on our state of mind.

How old are grandparents?

There are grandparents who are younger than fifty years of age, but most are in their sixties. They may seem young or old, depending on whether they see the proverbial glass as half empty or half full. For those who look on the bright side, life offers many joys and a great deal of satisfaction — not the least of which is enjoying the grandchildren.

Grandparents' health

Lack of physical activity at advanced ages is the greatest contributor to ill health. Regular exercise keeps both body and mind healthy and prolongs life. This doesn't mean deciding one day to take up tennis or jogging. Anyone who has not been exercising regularly should start slowly and be sure to consult a physician before undertaking a fitness program.

Grandparents' mental abilities

Although few sixty-year-olds can run and jump the way they did when they were twenty, there's no reason they can't live full intellectual lives. Picasso and Miro are two examples of artists who worked well into their nineties. Rubinstein was a famed concert pianist when he died at the age of eighty-seven. Michelangelo finished painting the Sistine Chapel when he was sixty-five. At sixty-eight, Cervantes finished the second part of *Don Quixote*. Verdi composed *Falstaff* when he was in his eighties, and Goethe finished *Faust* at the age of eighty-two.

What determines how well and how long grandparents live?

Food, exercise, and state of mind. Actually, these three factors are important all through life. But they are even more vital during late adulthood. It is important to have regular physical check-ups, an exercise program, and a good diet. A healthy life-style will mean a few sacrifices — less drinking and no smoking. And as for state of mind, it's important for all people to have work or hobbies they care about and an open mind to new ideas and new activities. A famous thinker was once asked, "What's a sure sign of old age?" And he replied, "Lack of curiosity."

The "golden years" begin around sixty and usually end in the seventies or eighties. But some people live to be over a hundred years of age.